It's Pumpkin Time
Little Farm

To my mom, Robin for all the special fall memories growing up.
— K.J.

Find our books at Amazon, Barnes & Nobles, Walmart, Books-A-Million, OverDrive, Kobo, Lulu and more!

Like, Share and Follow us on Facebook, Instagram, Twitter, Pinterest, YouTube, LinkedIn and more!

www.SlothDreams.com

Text Copyright© 2022 by KeriAnne N. Jelinek & Coral Jelinek
Illustrations copyright ©2022 KeriAnne N. Jelinek
Illustrations Licensed to Sloth Dreams Publishing LLC via Canva.com
All rights reserved, including the right of reproduction in whole are in part in any form.
Sloth Dreams Publishing and colophon are registered trademarks of Sloth Dreams Publishing LLC.

Published by Sloth Dreams Publishing
Sloth Dreams Children's Books
Pennsylvania, USA
www.SlothDreams.com

All Rights Reserved
ISBN: 978-8-2517-8777-2

Except in the United States of America, this book is sold subject to the condition that it shall not, by way of trade or otherwise, be lent, re-sold, hired out, or otherwise circulated without the publisher's prior consent in any form of binding or cover other that in which it is published and without a similar condition including this condition being imposed on the subsequent purchaser.

You know it's pumpkin time when the Little Farm wakes from its long sleep to a brisk and cool fall morning.

You know it's pumpkin time when the Little Farm sees geese flying south for the winter.

You know it's pumpkin time on the Little Farm when the farmer and his wife eat pumpkin pancakes with maple syrup for breakfast.

You know it's pumpkin time when you taste the crisp homemade apple cider from Little Farms' cider press.

You know it's pumpkin time on the Little Farm when leaves start to make a magical blanket of colors on the ground below.

You know it's pumpkin time on the Little Farm when the pumpkin patch has vines winding through pumpkins of every shape and size.

You know it's pumpkin time when the little red tractor at the Little Farm pulls the hayride full of moms, dads, and children out to the pumpkin patch.

You know it's pumpkin time when the big tractors begin to work in the fields from dawn until dusk on the Little Farm.

You know it's pumpkin time at the Little Farm when children run from the bus to the pumpkin patch to pick a pumpkin just the right size to take home.

You know it's pumpkin time when the animals of the Little Farm are taken in from the fields and are snug and warm in their cozy little red barn in their very own stables for the cool fall nights.

You know it's pumpkin time when the days begin to shorten, and the sun starts to set behind the hills of the pumpkin patch on the Little Farm.

You know it's pumpkin time on the Little Farm when bats come out at dusk to dine upon apples that have fallen to the ground below.

Find our books at Amazon, Barnes & Nobles, Walmart, Books-A-Million, OverDrive, Kobo, Lulu and more!

Like, Share and Follow us on Facebook, Instagram, Twitter, Pinterest, YouTube, LinkedIn and more!

www.SlothDreams.com

Text Copyright© 2022 by KeriAnne N. Jelinek & Coral Jelinek
Illustrations copyright ©2022 KeriAnne N. Jelinek
Illustrations Licensed to Sloth Dreams Publishing LLC via Canva.com
All rights reserved, including the right of reproduction in whole are in part in any form.
Sloth Dreams Publishing and colophon are registered trademarks of Sloth Dreams Publishing LLC.

Published by Sloth Dreams Publishing
Sloth Dreams Children's Books
Pennsylvania, USA
www.SlothDreams.com

All Rights Reserved
ISBN: 978-8-2517-8777-2

Except in the United States of America, this book is sold subject to the condition that it shall not, by way of trade or otherwise, be lent, re-sold, hired out, or otherwise circulated without the publisher's prior consent in any form of binding or cover other that in which it is published and without a similar condition including this condition being imposed on the subsequent purchaser.

www.ingramcontent.com/pod-product-compliance
Lightning Source LLC
LaVergne TN
LVHW070432070526
838199LV00014B/491